Notes from a Caregiver

Meg Lindsay

A Publication of The Poetry Box®

©2020 Meg Lindsay
All rights reserved.

Editing & Book Design by Shawn Aveningo Sanders
Cover Artwork: Painting by Meg Lindsay
Cover Design by Robert R. Sanders
Author Photo by Roy Weinstein

No part of this book may be reproduced in any manner
whatsoever without permission from the author, except
in the case of brief quotations embodied in critical essays,
reviews and articles.

ISBN: 978-1-948461-52-8
Printed in the United States of America.
Wholesale distribution via Ingram.

Published by The Poetry Box®, 2020
Portland, Oregon
ThePoetryBox.com

*For
those who suffer
and
their caregivers
and
for my husband whose resilience, insights,
and generosity to others
in the midst of his own collapse
continues to leave me
in awe*

In *Timaeus* 71-3, Plato explains that God mixed fire, water, air and earth to fashion bone marrow and create a "universal seed-stuff for every mortal kind."

Contents

Spotlit	7
Diagnosis	8
That First Stay in the Hospital	11
What They Don't Tell You	13
The Therapist Asks What Do I Feel?	15
Marigolds	16
After Denial	17
Bardo	19
Sherpa	20
Mornings	21
At Trader Joe's	22
Dawn Before the Stem Cell Harvest	24
Who He Is	25
Reclaiming His Life	26
Pain Scale	27
Driving Back from Lake Placid	28
In the Kitchen	30
Black Ice	31
Asterisk	32
Visible Signs	33
At the Subway Stop	35
Widows	36
Tarzan	37
Sketchbooks	38

Today	39
What I Miss	40
Gone at the Beach	41
Gary's Koan	42
In the Meditation Group	43
Notes & Acknowledgments	45
Praise for *Notes from Caregiver*	46
About the Author	49
About The Poetry Box®	50

Spotlit

The remaining leaves chatter
among themselves where he usually
sits on the deck in the sun while I paint inside.
Down by the river a train whistles
and I wonder at the containment
of my body and self in my skin, separate
from him yet merged. I sense when
his moods and numbers change. I startle
myself as I think I do not have cancer.
No. He has cancer but we
live together within his cancer,
in its spotlit conversation,
fraught with overtones
of endings that cancer is.

Words float, emotions seek to attach
like spiders sense when you leave,
come out to spin their webs
sticky silk from ceilings
into empty space.
A wildish black one, tiny
mini tarantula, darts erratic
across the window glass
barely noticeable light fiddle pattern
on its back. Black widow? I capture it
safe in a glass but it hops in fright, imprisoned
in the glass, take it away across
the road, hope it won't come back
to bite.

Diagnosis

1. To Create Order

The day after
my husband's diagnosis
multiple myeloma, cancer of plasma and bones
after weeks of watching his increasing pain
and not knowing why,
I know I have to
get to the Saturday morning municipal shredder
my private documents, solicitations from banks,
unnecessary, obsolete
statements from a defunct brokerage house,
to protect from anyone
who might rifle through our trash.
I sit, wait in line in my car as instructed,
as a sudden train howls its whistle
above my head on the trestle,
while I wait, alone, parked down below in the lot,
engine idling.

2. What To Say

Say
very ill.
Establishes a wall
the blandness of which
politeness hesitates to breach
so you don't have to explain
again
what kind of cancer
to those so shocked and ruffled,
whose angst needs to be soothed
and patted down.

3. Obliterate

The sound of his hands
reflexively rubbing
away the ache in his collapsing bones, in his chest.
Do something. Reinvent. Subvert
Trump's misogyny, his locker room talk,
the TV chatter.
Click of the wall switch off.
It's taking too long for my pupils to adjust.

4. Last Night

I'm sorry I'm sorry I'm sorry
he called, moaned in a spasm
having knocked the plastic cup with water
to the floor as it was late
when the pain is worse
and I'd moved from my own teary empathy
into anger, after driving him home
from the doctor and his howls
and yelps as over each bump
we go at 7 miles per hour, no, it is
not my fault, even though I am
driving the car.

5. For Days After

Is it ok to obsessively regret returning
a too short, fleece bathrobe to Kohl's, missing
the upside down, silly white sheep
who float in dark grey?
Won't show stains or tatters.
I could have been warm, loose, free
in soft fuzzy fleece
to run in meadows

[. . .]

with the impossibly white sheep
who float on their stiff stick legs,
each one watching, immobile,
frozen.

6. What They Say

They say *take care of yourself*
over and over
like there is a choice
after I help get his cereal into a bowl
in a way so he won't drop the spoon,
empty the portable urinals,
bathe his feet,
after doling out the day's allotment of pills,
pick up the dirty socks and pajamas,
get two cars serviced
remembering to alternate driving each
so the batteries won't die,
find a wheel chair at the medical facility,
push him to his hour long infusion.

7. Fear of Drowning

sink slowly as
waves disappear
into occasional crests,
sift and evolve, evolve
and sift but
while sinking
think I will never . . .
again . . .

That First Stay in the Hospital

—I remember the tall computer stands the nurses wheeled from room to room, and how every few hours they asked my husband for his name and date of birth, and I remember being glad I wasn't responsible for such complicated things as drugs that might save his life.

—I don't remember his three consecutive roommates as they were all loud and only a curtain between but I do remember the annoyance of my husband, who survived in spite of their keeping the TV on 24/7.

—I remember when the first roommate moved out and I hastily solicited the head nurse to claim the now empty bed by the window, illusion of space with its view of the tops of trees he could see looking up from his pillow to the vastness of blue sky.

—I can't remember the names of the twenty-some drugs the attending physician enumerated, standing next to my husband's bed, late that tenth day in the hospital, she Eastern European with a thick accent that was hard for me to understand, and we both tired, she looking as miserable as me, hot in spite of the hospital a/c, having to go through each drug in detail, complicated five syllable names loaded with 'x's and 'z's. No one had told me I would be responsible in order for him to be released, and that later I'd have to create a spread sheet to keep it straight.

—I remember restless nights, my heart thumping too fast, that tenth day going back twice into the dim light of Sam's Club, the long walk on a hard, concrete floor through boxes of children's diapers and porch furniture and plastic plants, clutching the corrected prescriptions to override the phoned in mistakes. I remember panicking, not finding someone to help move the heavy sofa so the hospital bed could be delivered.

[. . .]

—I am not sure I remember the first time I had a sip of that beet and lemon ginger smoothie in the lobby of the new cancer center as I waited for my husband to complete his first, or was it the fourth, day of radiation while his younger brother, a 61-year old CEO from Virginia, did business on his cell. I do remember it cost $7.95 and thinking irritably it must be a profit center for the hospital, and the name ZINGER and the sharp tang on my tongue, the vibrancy I felt from that drink, the coolness, a reprieve from the glare of hot summer sun. At home I sometimes try to replicate that ZINGER, unsuccessfully, even though I had written each ingredient down on a receipt.

What They Don't Tell You

After 10 days in a hospital
you regain the ability
to walk albeit with a cane so I put the commode
out in the hall as you are laughing a bit more,
the gleam back, but the chemo starts
and the next morning again pain
in your ribs and sternum
and now it burns
in your chest and again you
can't make it up the stairs.
A spasm and your body folds into itself,
into the sign of the crab.

No one tells us there is a
spray guard to insert in the commode.
No one says do not go off
stool softeners while on pain killers
even if things get loose.
No one tells you so we don't know if what seemed
an upward trend is reversing,
no, no, not the wrong way
back to where you were
at its worst when we didn't know
what it was.

They don't tell you
what to expect, maybe because
seeing so many, they don't have time
or maybe no writers on the medical staff to make inclusive lists
or if they told you the range of options, maybe
they fear the details will break you.
No one is willing to tell you anything firm except
multiple myeloma has 900 gene variations,
multiple myeloma is incurable

[. . .]

although it can be blocked,
although undetected weeds smolder.
Not remission, not as in *remit, to cancel or refrain
from exacting or inflicting (a debt or punishment)*?
No one tells you that, after 36 years of marriage,
you are about to spend
the most intimate moments of your life
with this man and his body.

The Therapist Asks What Do I Feel

like I'm in Scotland, mellow
walking out of a pub
and I am looking left but
the truck comes from the right
and hits me
splat
broadside
skittering parts of me in all directions
because the rules of this road are different

his decline and cascading pain
before diagnosis
bam

and I keep on
but the truck backs up over me
shifting its gears
as the diagnosis hits
like a big bam

then the chemo
bam

pervasive muffled creeping poisons
every day throughout the day,
little
    bam bam bam

Marigolds

I buy the last box of 6 marigolds.
Two are broken, their orange blossoms
lost but for $2.49 it doesn't
seem to matter. I don't buy
the large hibiscus we usually get
for our condo deck, for privacy, for love
of the lush pink into purples,
because he had always potted and cared for them,
carried those heavy plants to the front
for our neighbor to water when we drove
off to Maine lobster or Cape Cod beaches
and grandchildren. I can't take on more carrying,
more cleaning, more laundry,
nor water another plant but I can bring
marigolds home and dig little holes
near the garage door in anticipation
that some of the blooms might thrive,
to catch a glimpse of the color I miss
on canvasses, which I've no time to pull out,
these warm summer months, my painting time.
The broken plants revive, hints of orange unfold
as dazzlingly bright. But parts of the soil must be loaded
with something bad, as ones nearest
the foundation slowly wither.

After Denial

White hot anger, seething, sops up
my disintegrating generosity.
Anger at his spasms.
Anger at his looking at me stupidly
when I tell him again for the third time
that he agreed to call the pharmacy
for the reference number for the rejected
prescription of oxy (which pill he just took)
that is not in his insurance formulary
for which his palliative care RN asked
by 10 AM this morning.
Anger at his walking 20 minutes
with a cane, twice in the day, outside
sometimes strong enough to forget to use the cane
but at night, he's worse and sits, waiting
for me to make him dinner.
Anger that once made, he wants
me to carry it to him.
Anger that, swollen feet sweating,
he leaves his dirty socks alongside
the crumpled tissues on the table,
all of which he seems able to ignore.
Anger that he sits stolid, irrefutable
in the middle of where I paint, rather painted,
when I had the time to paint.
Anger that anger is destroying my ability
to care for him with a smile, with healing
like Tom Brokaw's wife in his book.
Anger that we hunger for any sign
of less pain, of his being able
to put pants on himself, without hands shaking
and those shallow breaths.
Anger that spots of scaly red
have appeared on my forearms and itch

[. . .]

like pin pricks into my soul.
Anger that, a friend was right,
our "lives have exploded"
and I don't know how to get them back.

Bardo

Death is a dash
or could it be
death is a circular particularity
as in the dot at the top of the semicolon,
its paired comma, a wave,
a sweeping away
along the coastline blue?

Death as a question mark
would be hackneyed beyond belief
(we are not talking belief here),
not even close to the tensed form
of a mongoose alert at dawn
eyes sharp for food, or is it foe?

But death as a broader space?
Not empty dash or semicolon,
not the finality of the period,
but a lull, Bardo, a Buddhist gap lengthening,
a slowing of a breath,
no panic of the abyss,
just those layers, as taught, leveling into light.
Theoretically.

Sherpa

I carry two pillows, one to soften
where his collapsed vertebrae touch the back of a chair
and the other, a thicker Tempur-Pedic
to cushion the bones of his butt.
I carry the water bottle
from the cyclist's shop where he used to buy
his racing gear, because his mouth gets dry
from the pills and to take a painkiller
if whatever we are doing becomes
too much. I carry the walker from the garage
to the car. I push the metal buttons down
in order to swing shut the sides, slowly
so the wheels don't catch
and get stuck as that time when I couldn't
get them open at the medical facility,
the line of cars growing as the valet driver
waited for our keys and handicap sign.
I carry cash, our phones, credit cards
and his medical information
and a sweater for him and one for me.
I carry our food.
I carry a heaviness that I can't
seem to leave behind. It lives somewhere
inside my skull, my eyes, not visible
except on those occasions
when someone asks how I am.

Mornings

I refuse to go downstairs
for at least a half hour
with no early doctor's appointment to get him to
so I stay in bed, like Edith Wharton (without her maid
to pick up the pages), my pen inking its way
through the picayune specificities of the days before,
page after scribbled illegible page.

Oh, I so hope this all some day becomes memory.
It seems there will never be anything else but this
although my rational mind says, as another friend suggests,
yes, this too shall pass.

But then as I creep barefoot into my office,
I hear him downstairs with his cane, clumping about
and a clink of the spoon on his glass cereal bowl
as he gets his own breakfast,
he, knowing, he too wanting to give me a few moments,
an unspoken agreement, among so many,
before that other kind of day unfolds.

At Trader Joe's

As I stand, stuck behind the flow of lettuce,
organic eggs and box of precooked rice,
I notice the older cashier I'd passed by,
moves fast, much faster, and indeed I am stuck, slowed down
but relieved to be so slowed, with an earache throbbing,
sharp pain stabbing, only occasional
now after the doctor's visit but my weepiness is increasing
oddly with less pain, so that I am happy,
almost peaceful, to be stuck in a line
with nothing to do but inch along.
I watch as the older clerk in jeans and flowered shirt
asks his customer, an older Asian woman, wide face
set in a scowl, short hair cut tight, he asks
while putting her large plant into her cart
"Do you speak English?" and she looks blank.
"Do you speak Korean?" as he hoists up
clusters of cucumbers and beets
and she looks from side to side, as if considering,
slides past me to bring back a young Asian woman,
and he says, "I just wanted to wish her a good day in Korean,"
and smiles and words I cannot not understand dance in the air.
Then, the by-now-I-assume-daughter bows,
"No, we are Japanese" and he repeats after her in Japanese
and again the three smile and formally bow
and by then my groceries are bagged, lightly
by the young man who had asked me
to lift one, to see if it was too heavy.
I push my cart across the bumpy lot,
place the not-too-heavy paper bags
in the back, and sit in my car and weep at the pain
in my ear that I cannot control, at the kindness of my cashier,
at the warmth of the older cashier,
at the doctor I've known for years
who squeezed me in that same day

and gave me a free sample of expensive medicine to squirt
up my right nostril to reach the swelling in my inner ear,
and at the idea dawning on me after six months
that my once athletic husband is forever changed, as am I,
and we do not know where this leads.

Dawn Before Stem Cell Harvest

*In the Helmsley Medical Tower/ New York City Hotel
for Patients and Hospital Staff*

the view from the 8th floor down onto an empty street,
sea of silent dark except for the few circles of gold under street
    lamps,
catty corner and up, the glass facade of a building,
not flat, not unlike my husband's rearranged version of his spine
bent at odd angles, a zigzag wave
dotted with odd shadows that move
behind the glass, randomly lit,
office night workers

dawn imperceptibly inching forward
a few figures on the sidewalks—
phlebotomists, oncologists, physiatrists, PA's, RN's—
trickle into the bowels below us, ants tunneling in

numbers increasing on either side
of a single line of yellow cabs,
headlights still on, car after car,
relentless, all only in one direction
into somewhere underneath us,
although we know this one way street

dead ends into the East River,
these taxis carrying patients, adrenalin flowing,
some who will die this day,
some who will receive a reprieve

and the last night lights dissolve
into the blaze of an emerging sun
as the zigzag wall of glass
becomes, once again, unreadable,
behind its reflection of clouds and blue.

Who He Is

He wants to ski downhill,
a lifetime of dancing down snow bumps but now
he's not supposed to lift over 10 pounds one doctor said,
and another said 20. I bring up
his boots and skis and take off my shoes to stand
on our glass digital scale while he hands me first
each boot and then the two skis and those weigh
twenty-three point six pounds
without the poles.
Up north the snow has melted and frozen again.
Crunch, crunch the sound of boots on hard pack.
His doctors say *don't fall.*

Reclaiming His Life

At the multiple myeloma meeting in front of 15 survivors
after he describes his rapid decline—
the 5 or more ribs broken, his permanently deformed sternum
and compressed vertebrae fractures—
he, sheepish as a guilty boy, admits
to the silence of even this battered group,
stunned by the degree of his breakage
that has left him bent and dependent on a cane,
that the day before he'd hit 100 golf balls
at the driving range,
something he'd not dared to say to me.
The spine specialist had said
ok if the correct form, but had not said
100 and that night indeed he'd complained
of the usual severe fatigue
and chronic pain and the *when will I ever feel better's*—
as if I might get annoyed,
which I am.

Pain Scale

Asked yet again if 1 to 10, the scientist in him
asks of what? His annoyance at the stupidity
of the pain scale itself, such lack
of nuanced dimension.

Before cancer he lived in philosophical angst,
a soul-deep bafflement about being born,
about work, about a failure to achieve
otherworldliness.

When his biofeedback teacher says
he is not ill, that he has a condition,
he detaches into new openness,
laughs often.

I decide we cannot know another.

He stops opiates when others cannot.
Doctors say his will to live is strong.
He says if it comes back,
he would not take treatment.

Driving Back from Lake Placid

I keep looking over at him in the passenger seat
slumped down awkwardly,
his jaw slack, lips parted,
and I am debating
if he's died, if finally his heart decided
enough, but that would mean I have
a dead person, a body next to me in the front seat.
What do you do with a dead person?
What if he's not dead? I should get him to a hospital
but he would kill me, if I took him to a hospital
and he really had died and I was responsible
for having him revived. So many bones broken,
so much nerve damage, so many warnings
that the cancer will come back—
a future of more lesions, more broken bones,
more chemo, more misery.
But if I don't take him to a hospital, am I
a murderer? Culpable? How long am I allowed
to drive around before I am culpable?
An hour? Three?
And after three hours, should I
drive straight to a funeral home?
Would that be presumptuous?
What is the proper sequence
of these things I never have dealt
with before?
He still does not move. It's been half an hour.
My heart beats fast and I look at the gas tank
thinking it might determine
how long I drive around.
We are an hour from home
and I'd so like to be home.
He stirs, gulps air, blinks and asks
how close are we. Later he agrees

he would have killed me
if I'd had him revived and he'd missed
an easy out.

In the Kitchen

I'm cooking.
I don't like cooking, cooking alone
the shrimp he likes and he, tired,
coming back late, I can tell
he's aching, but he knows I'm hungry, senses
I'm tired and anxiously starts to help
so I spill the green smoothie I'm pouring from a blender
after I've caught sight of him getting up on a stool,
to reach a bottle of wine for cooking the shrimp
and I'm freaked he'll fall
so I banish him from the kitchen and he says he knows
I'm stressed and he wants to help but I know
he's stressed and must go upstairs
and lie down and we both must back off
but he's shaky and I yell
because he wants to help and he yells
and none of this is working.

Black Ice

In the dark I sprinkle fine sand
over a broad swatch of black water
that has frozen slick and shiny,
and shout, because he's far off in the parking lot,
to point out where I've sanded
so he won't slip
but he doesn't stop, poles his way,
uses hiking poles to push evenly up against
his bent upper back to breathe better,
muscles ahead, choosing not to hear,
onto the ice and beyond
like he used to bushwhack
hiking in the high peaks.
Standing there in the street light,
left behind holding a heavy canister of sand,
I realize we have two different agendas,
his to live full out
and mine to keep him safe.

Asterisk

Notice of the report
pops up in his emails
two weeks after we'd thought
the annual PET MRI was clear
for another year. Instead we read
lesions in the brain
in the *Impressions Section*
says *similar to,*
similar to what? Past
or predictive of our future?
And *lesions in osseous*
but also maybe similar
so we see *lesions* and *brain*
where we'd rather not
see *similar* to anything at all and I
start ironing, make creases where there
were none, force scalding steam
into the cotton to make it smooth,
eradicate the crease I just fumbled in by mistake,
pointing the hot metal tip of the iron
into the wrong place,
each sizzling turn, too hot to touch,
creates a pattern.

Visible Signs

The physician's assistant says
as she clicks the mouse
as she stares at the blue screen
oh he'll want to resume chemo

and we are torn
between chemo, side effects,
the new immunotherapies
or
an emptiness
perhaps sooner, or rather later

and the oncologist says
it's change, it's what we've expected,
from .05 to .20,
you've done no maintenance
to keep it down and we counter with
he's healed his broken bones,
not built up resistance to the drugs
and the oncologist says
we'll do another test

so I ask him about his Thanksgiving,
wanting him to pause, wanting him not to vanish
behind a closing door and he says
he is *cooking, two cranberry sauces so far,*
one with chutney and I say *I prefer to add orange.*

Does he see beyond our unchanging expressions
the bomb lobbed
into our lives
as we try to think
what more to ask before he shuts the door

as we sit and look at him
as he looks at the screen
as his hand, each time, clicks the mouse,
moves the mouse, searching?

At the Subway Stop
after Ezra Pound

He walks bent,
a wrecked apparition
that clumps
flicking forward hiking poles
for balance. Faces
turn nervously toward him
as he approaches
and the crowd parts
like petals that flutter
before a wind,
their black unease.

Widows

That's what widows do:
withdraw, fold

their wings unto themselves
to seek that lost part.

They hide all winter in their caves
except she comes out, her eyes

glazed grey like his
when I last saw him outside.

She walks her fluffy
small dog, the kind with the pointy nose

and we talk about the sleet
or when will snow end

and if I stay too long,
she starts to tap into

the morass of her anger at the doctors,
her anger at the hospital

and at the husband who refused
early surgery, echoes

my husband's misdiagnosis, recalls
a future I do not wish to see.

Tarzan

For another 5 weeks, his numbers
are ok, only a brief skirmish,
don't require resumption of treatment
even though PET scan stirrings
  —hypermetabolic—
a warm spot as vague as melancholia
radiating on his iliac and its crest.

This gap we live in—
the couple who can't return calls,
the man who tells me in the grocery aisle
he doesn't know how to talk to sick people—
but I don't either,
don't know how to talk
to us, am bitchy.

I'd like to grab a tree vine,
push off like Tarzan,
sinewy arms and legs wrapped 'round
to swing, swish free
pass over this chasm below
not instead, a suspension,
a lack of momentum,

as we dangle in a mindless
erratic spin—not clear where
to want to land, two lives
in limbo waiting on destiny's
twirl, we clumsily wobbling tops
in our ever diminishing circles,
losing momentum
yet each moment, choice,
as if we have choice.

Sketchbooks

...mine, neglected
many and varied size,
each the last half or so blank,
stopped at my fill of a subject
—owls, cows, turkey buzzards—
ready for their leap onto canvas,
each sketch the blackist 6B lead crumbles
into the grab of paper's tooth,
random wild questionings fall off the page,
keys to a larger but at a slant

not precisely composed nor perfectly framed
within the confines of four edges,
not each book filled,
not orderly, nor complete

while that sketch from Lake Placid—
my husband charcoaled into his lawn chair
his vertebrae not yet crumpled,
the view to the Gothics range
as 8 foot sunflowers
wave their silly heads in high peak winds,
spill off the page askew—
the paper its own color, intrudes—
clouds, shifting

Today

my husband's laugh has a touch
of wildness
or is it madness
having peered into the abyss

What I Miss

I miss his walk without pain.
I miss the freedom with which
    he danced on skis
    down bump slopes
and I miss not worrying
    if he's fatigued,
    if he hurts more than the day before
    as he walks,
    his spine curved and bent.
    (Did we forget pillows if the restaurant chairs
    have a hard rim that might cut
    into his back?)
I miss an earlier time when if I made a mistake,
    it would not mean more broken bones
    or saving his life.
I miss the years thinking our marriage
    won't work out
    and my dread of becoming a caregiver
    —so expected of daughter, sister, wife—
    now that I am
    (and worrying he would be too self-involved
    to take care of me).
I miss all our previous petty innocences,
    before facing head on, his utter collapse
    and threat of death and I miss
    not realizing how
    deeply entwined we've become, so the giving
    of care becomes the seamless give and take
    of sameness of self.

Gone at the Beach

Living with someone with cancer in remission
is being distracted, like at a Maine beach in June,
its bright umbrellas, variety of flesh
and bodies emerged from winter's
cocoon, pale or burnt,
skinny stick figures, round short, round tall,
pudgy babies in floppy hats, one cradled
on a man's belly transferred to mom's
sandy chest. Men's baggy bathing suits,
drippy clingy to the thighs barely hanging on
beneath the bulge of a paunch and that gaggle
of leggy teenage girls, clustered, coltish in spring,
while the lone golden goddess with long blond hair
flung back down to the small of her back
seemingly unaware, a string of a wedge of a thong
between muscular buttocks, glowing tan as she strides
purposefully along the tidal line
which is beginning to shift, to recede,
to spread back out to sea and the slender lady in her beach chair
reading in half a foot of water, marvelous
thick white hair looped on top of her head, the breeze
playing loose strands, clipped with a tortoise barrette,
feels the water has abandoned
her toes, wriggling exposed
in the coolness of damp sand. The long buried
emerge—the sharp edge of scallop shells, the glow
of broken sea glass, sand's infinite grains' migrations
like cell mutations—
imperceptible, unstoppable.

Gary's Koan

—you're cheerful! how do you do that?
—do you need evidence? it's sad if you need evidence to be cheerful
—because then you would be sad

—does this count as intimacy?
—sad that you have to ask

—instead of laughing, it sounds sad
—ha
—ho ho ho

—so, would you tell me who you are?
—I would tell you if I knew who I was
—You've had 74 years. A slow learner

In the Meditation Group

In the meditation group
my husband speaks of acceptance
but he doesn't mention his back has been broken,
doesn't say how many vertebrae—six or so—
which would have gotten their attention

but he obliquely mentions acceptance can be applied
to other things like suffering and death
and I wonder if those listening knew how close he'd come,
they would get chills in their spines,
grateful not to be him, his dread, his pain,
his cells mutating out of control.

They tell us to keep the eyes open in meditation,
important to experience
the full range of the world in all its display.
Myself, become an aperture into the sky,
an occasional emptiness of mind,
not to fill an opening
but to stay.

Notes & Acknowledgments

Multiple myeloma is not well known (not to be confused with melanoma, a cancer of skin cells) and is different from most cancers. It is cancer of the blood that forms in a type of white blood cell called a plasma cell. These cancer cells accumulate in the bone marrow, crowding out normal plasma cells, leading to lesions and bone breaks.

Considered treatable but incurable, early diagnosis is the key to reduce bone damage. The trigger for the genetic damage is not well known, though there are likely environmental and hereditary components. 9/11 responders have shown significantly higher incidence of multiple myeloma than the regular population suggesting exposure to toxic materials as a factor.

Grateful acknowledgment is made to the following publications where these poems or earlier versions of them first appeared:

> *Intima: A Journal of Narrative Medicine*: "Visible Signs" and "Driving" ("Driving Home from Lake Placid")
>
> *Light: A Journal of Photography and Poetry*: "Pain Scale"
>
> *Months to Years*: "That First Stay in the Hospital"
>
> *Pulse: Voices from the Heart of Medicine*: "What They Don't Tell You"
>
> *Still You — Poems of Illness and Healing* (Wolf Ridge Press): "Black Ice"
>
> *Tiferet Journal*: "Diagnosis"

Praise for
Notes from a Caregiver

In *Notes from a Caregiver*, Meg Lindsay reveals the deep truth about what happens in a woman's world, inner and outer, when her husband and life-partner is diagnosed with multiple myeloma, cancer of plasma and bones. With white-hot honesty and emotional clarity, she faces into the authentic core of her experience.

In the midst of a deeply personal, life-altering crisis, Ms. Lindsay engages the authority of a skilled and practiced poet to show us the effects of this illness upon patient, caregiver-life partner, and the deep bond at the core of a long-tern marriage. She uses her personal struggle to come to terms with the trauma contained in her experience to guide us into and through the difficult transformations, which occur when one is confronted with the challenges of living with cancer, be she, or he, patient or caregiver.

Notes from a Caregiver is a 'must read' for anyone, caregiver, patient, family member, or friend, who finds herself or himself in the chaos of a critical illness. I wish I had had it to accompany me when I was the primary caregiver for my husband in similar circumstances. In addition, as a psychotherapist in private practice, I see Meg Lindsay's book of poems as a guide for medical professionals, psychotherapists, and technicians, who treat people suffering from life-threatening illnesses, and their families. We can all become more educated to the sensitivities, and vulnerabilities, of the psychic shock that comes with this territory.

Just as Dante called upon Virgil, his poet-ancestor, to guide him into and through the Inferno, so Meg Lindsay calls on her own poetic genius to accompany her, and then she, in turn, carries us in and through the *Valley of the Shadow of Death* and beyond.

—Bonnie L. Damron, PhD, LCSW
Archetypal Pattern Analyst

When a wife suddenly becomes her husband's caregiver, everything changes—"because the rules of this road are different." In poems that are brutally realistic and deeply tender, poet and painter Meg Lindsay tells us what it's like when this new road is traveled. When her husband, collapsed with aggressive Multiple Myeloma, neither was prepared for the journey ahead. Just as Doctor William Carlos Williams wrote poems in between patients, Lindsay writes in exam rooms and waiting rooms, writes as her husband receives infusions and endures tests—and her poems tell of a new marital intimacy, one that emerged from the physical tending required by bed bath and commode, and from the emotional support demanded by a spouse's pain and disabilities. These are important and moving poems, beautifully transparent, and a roadmap for others who may be walking this same unfamiliar path.

—Cortney Davis, author of *Taking Care of Time*
(Winner, Wheelbarrow Poetry Prize, University of Michigan Press)

Through her capacity for deep and sustained attention, Meg Lindsay has transformed the burdens of caregiving into a strange sort of beauty. Small, painfully human moments and mundane tasks reverberate with profound meaning. We can feel Lindsay using language to heal the rupture that illness has created, and thus, her poetry becomes a salve for all of us, who will inevitably experience the suffering of someone we love. *Notes from a Caregiver* offers comfort, companionship, wisdom, and even humor, to those on caregiving's arduous journey. Lindsay's writing teaches us that to look closely and to struggle to put what we see and experience into words, is a powerful form of love.

—Charlotte Friedman, Adjunct Professor,
Narrative Medicine, Barnard College, Columbia University

Meg Lindsay's poems are deeply moving and sometimes even humorous. Each verse guides us through the twists and turns of a bone cancer diagnosis too late to avert injury, treatment, repair. Her words gently illuminate the arduous road she and her husband are

[...]

traveling and the continuous dialog between caregiver and patient. Their unrelenting partnership and love offer us a way forward.

> —Jen Walker, Attorney, Literacy Advocate
> and Multiple Myeloma Caregiver

This new collection, *Notes from a Caregiver* by Meg Lindsay, is laden with imagistic gems which brave the paradox of hope, when the "facts" are not in your favor. But there remains hope to this author, and hopelessness, inexpressible will and work and grief—all as true as any "fact." Lindsay writes "Death is a dash/or could it be.... Theoretically." I love the provocative questions which Lindsay insists be answered—answered with a dash—

This is a large-hearted, beautifully sequenced, well-crafted, and careful collection.

> —Kate Knapp Johnson, poet, author of *The Wind-Bike*

"These poems are fierce, passionate paeans to love—love of self and love for a beloved husband whose sickness has interfered but not destroyed the intensity of the relationship."

> —Julie Bondanza, Jungian Analyst

About the Author

A semi-finalist in two "Discovery"/The Nation Contests and a finalist in an Inkwell competition, Meg Lindsay has had poems published in *Tricycle, Pivot, Salamander, Alimentum, Connecticut River Review*, etc. and earned an MFA in poetry from Sarah Lawrence College.

Because she is also an established painter showing for decades in galleries and museums, her chapbook about the emotions and difficulties of painting, *A Painter's Night Journal*, was published by Finishing Line Press in 2016. Writers love to write about paintings, but most writers confine themselves to the subject matter of a painting, not the process, since after all most do not paint.

The subject of her writing dramatically changed direction when her husband, an athlete never ill before, collapsed with cancer in his bones, multiple myeloma, that same year. She gained direct knowledge of what it means to be a caregiver, a different and extraordinarily difficult learning process from anything she had ever known before.

<www.meglindsayartist.com>

About The Poetry Box®

The Poetry Box® is a boutique publishing company that enjoys providing a platform for both established and emerging poets to share their words with the world through beautiful printed books and chapbooks.

Feel free to visit the online bookstore (thePoetryBox.com), where you'll find more titles including:

Psyche's Scroll by Karla Linn Merrifield

November Quilt by Penelope Scambly Schott

Shrinking Bones by Judy K. Mosher

Fireweed by Gurdrun Bortman

Surreal Expulsion by D.R. James

Impossible Ledges by Dianne Avey

Abruptio by Melissa Fournier

Like the O in Hope by Jeanne Julian

What She Was Wearing by Shawn Aveningo Sanders

Moroccan Holiday by Lauren Tivey

Shadow Man by Margaret Chula

A Long, Wide Stretch of Calm by Melanie Green

The Very Rich Hours by Gregory Loselle

and more . . .

www.ingramcontent.com/pod-product-compliance
Lightning Source LLC
LaVergne TN
LVHW090040080526
838202LV00046B/3889